ROSEN Verified

THE BILL OF RIGHTS

What Is the Right to a Trial by Jury?

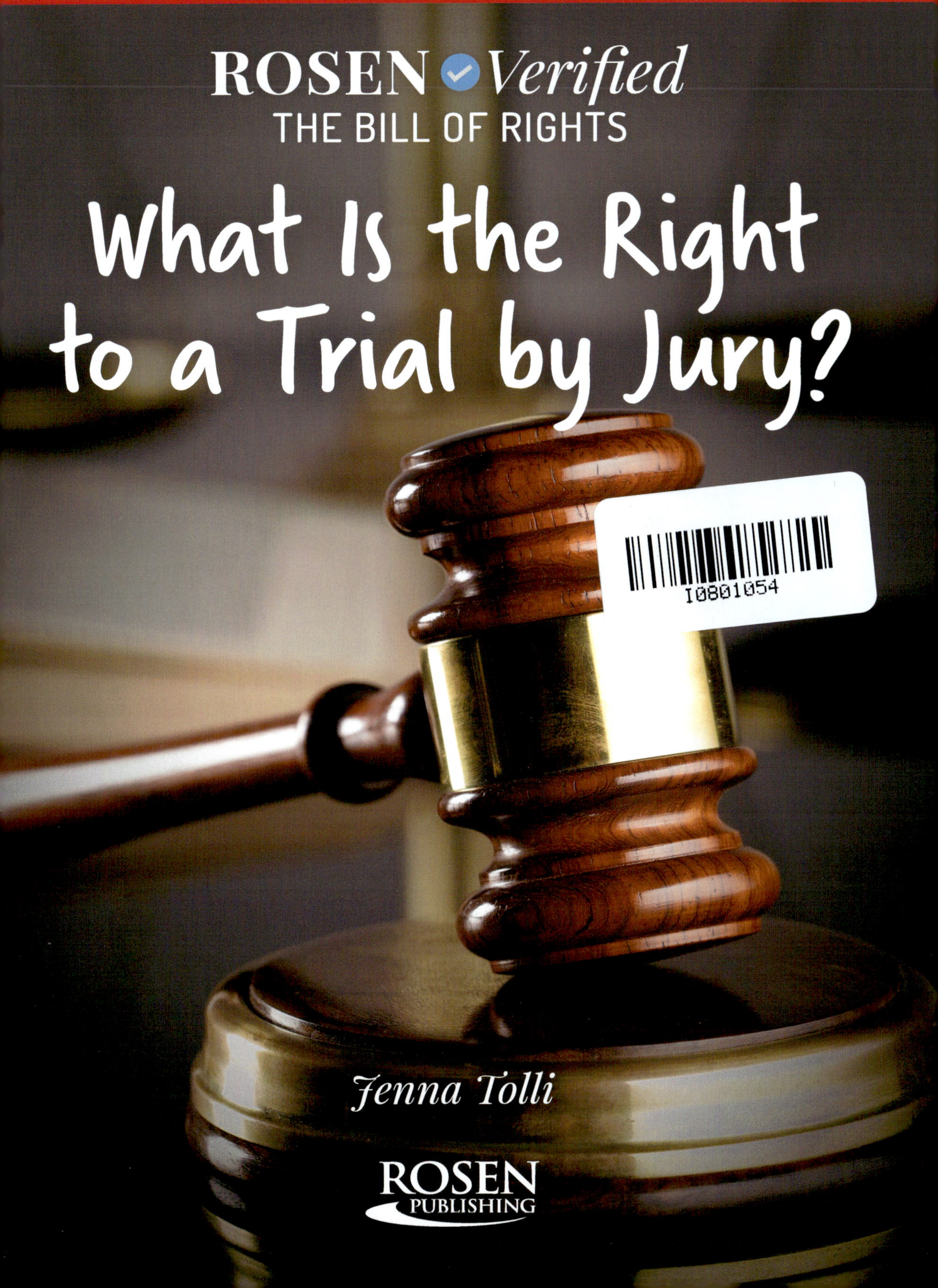

Jenna Tolli

ROSEN PUBLISHING

Published in 2024 by The Rosen Publishing Group, Inc.
2544 Clinton Street, Buffalo, NY 14224

First Edition

Editor: Greg Roza
Book Design: Michael Flynn

Photo Credits: Cover Zolnierek/Shutterstock.com; (series background) PinkPueblo/Shutterstock.com; pp. 5, 28-29 sirravelalot/Shutterstock.com; p. 7 larry1235/Shutterstock.com; p. 9 Everett Collection/Shutterstock.com; p. 11 hbpro/Shutterstock.com; p. 13 Nolichuckyjake/Shutterstock.com; p. 14 LifetimeStock/Shutterstock.com; p. 15 fizkes/Shutterstock.com; pp. 17, 37 Gorodenkoff/Shutterstock.com; p. 19 SaiArLawKa2/Shutterstock.com; p. 21 Pixel-Shot/Shutterstock.com; p. 23 wavebreakmedia/Shutterstock.com; pp. 24-25 B Brown/Shutterstock.com; p. 27 Africa Studio/Shutterstock.com; p. 31 Gorodenkoff/Shutterstock.com; p. 33 Rosamar/Shutterstock.com; p. 35 Junial Enterprises/Shutterstock.com; p. 39 Salivanchuk Semen/Shutterstock.com; p. 41 Kzenon/Shutterstock.com; p. 42 Studio Romantic/Shutterstock.com; p. 43 MR.Yanukit/Shutterstock.com; p. 45 5 second Studio/Shutterstock.com.

Cataloging-in-Publication Data

Names: Tolli, Jenna.
Title: What is the right to a trial by jury? / Jenna Tolli.
Description: New York : Rosen Publishing, 2024. | Series: Rosen verified: the Bill of Rights | Includes glossary and index.
Identifiers: ISBN 9781499469752 (pbk.) | ISBN 9781499469769 (library bound) | ISBN 9781499469776 (ebook)
Subjects: LCSH: United States. Constitution. 6th Amendment--Juvenile literature. | United States. Constitution. 7th Amendment--Juvenile literature. | United States. Constitution. 1st-10th Amendments--Juvenile literature. | Jury--United States--Juvenile literature. | Fair trial--United States--Juvenile literature. | Right to counsel--United States--Juvenile literature. | Due process of law--United States--Juvenile literature.
Classification: LCC KF8972.T65 2024 | DDC 345.73'056--dc23

Manufactured in the United States of America

Some of the images in this book illustrate individuals who are models. The depictions do not imply actual situations or events.

CPSIA Compliance Information: Batch #CSRYA24. For further information contact Rosen Publishing at 1-800-237-9932.

CONTENTS

Right to a Trial Jury

The U.S. Constitution, which is the law of the land, was created to **protect** the rights and freedoms of U.S. citizens. The country was founded on the belief that people are created equal (although what "people" means has changed). Everyone should have fundamental, or basic, rights.

If someone is accused of, or blamed for, a crime or wrongdoing, they may have a trial. A trial is a meeting in a court in which **evidence** is given to the judge and often a jury. A jury is a group of people chosen to make a decision in a legal, or law, case.

Trial juries are an important part of our **democracy** and legal system. People who are accused of crimes need to have their rights protected. They also need to have laws applied fairly. Before someone can be **convicted** of a crime, they have the right to have their case heard by a group of their peers. This can help avoid unfair convictions.

The Sixth **Amendment** and Seventh Amendment give people the right to have a trial jury if they are accused of a crime or wrongdoing.

Trial juries are made up of six to twelve people. They are also known as petit juries. "Petit" means small.

Constitution and Bill of Rights

Article 3 of the Constitution gives U.S. citizens the right to a trial by jury. When the Constitution was written, however, some people felt it didn't give citizens enough protections. James Madison used these ideas to write a list of amendments to the Constitution. The states later **ratified** 10 of these amendments. These amendments are now known as the Bill of Rights.

The Sixth Amendment and Seventh Amendment protect different **aspects** of trials and juries. They also give protections for people accused of committing, or doing, crimes.

AMENDMENT MATH

James Madison originally proposed a list of 19 amendments to Congress. Congress approved 12, but two of the amendments weren't approved by the states.

VERIFIED

You can read the Constitution and Bill of Rights on the U.S. Congress website: **www.congress.gov/founding-documents**.

The Constitution went into effect in March 1789, and the amendments were sent to the states in October 1789. The amendments that make up the Bill of Rights were ratified in December 1791.

History of Juries

In England from the 1400s to 1600s, people faced unfair conditions during trials. Defendants didn't always have the chance to have their case heard and then often received unfair **sentences**.

It was important to the Founding Fathers that trials in the United States should be conducted fairly. They said decisions would be made by a group of citizens rather than just by the government. Juries have been an important part of our democracy since the country was founded.

PEOPLE IN THE COURT

Defendant: The person or group accused of breaking the law or doing something wrong.

Judge: The public official who presides over, or hears, cases.

Lawyer: A professional who has studied law and handles lawsuits, or law cases. They may also be called an attorney.

Plaintiff: The person against whom a crime has been done, or the people of the state itself. The prosecution is the person or legal team that brings legal action in a court of law.

It wasn't until the Civil Rights Act of 1957 that women were given the right to serve on federal, or national, juries.

Trial by Jury

The Sixth Amendment says that in all criminal cases, the person accused of the crime should have a "speedy and public trial, by an impartial [fair] jury."

The first part of the amendment is to make sure people don't spend too much time in jail before having a trial. If someone hasn't yet been convicted of a crime, they shouldn't have to spend a long time behind bars.

Waiting a long time between charges and trial can also mean that evidence could be lost before the trial. It might also be harder to find witnesses, and these witnesses may not remember things as well.

FAMOUS WORDS

Thomas Jefferson once wrote, "I consider the trial by jury as the only anchor [connection] ever yet imagined by man by which a government can be held to the **principles** of its constitution."

The Speedy Trial Act of 1974 limits the amount of time between different stages of a court case. It states a trial needs to start within 70 days.

Public Trials

The Sixth Amendment also gives the right to public trials. A trial usually takes place in the same district where the crime took place. A district is the geographic area, or place, that the court handles.

There are times when a judge needs to move the trial location, like when there is a lot of media attention about the crime. If a juror has heard about the case, they might form their own view of it. This could mean it wouldn't be a fair trial.

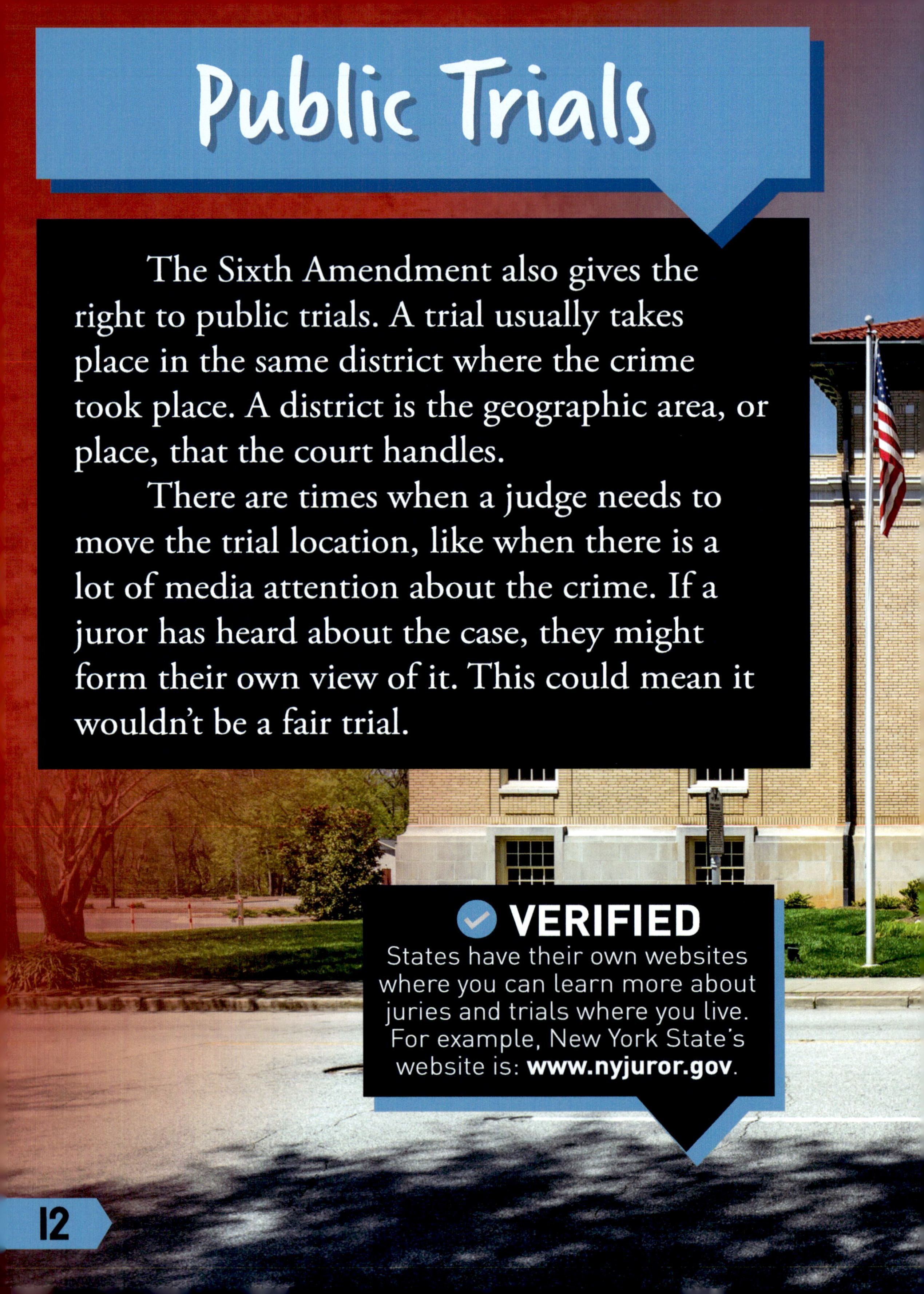

VERIFIED

States have their own websites where you can learn more about juries and trials where you live. For example, New York State's website is: **www.nyjuror.gov**.

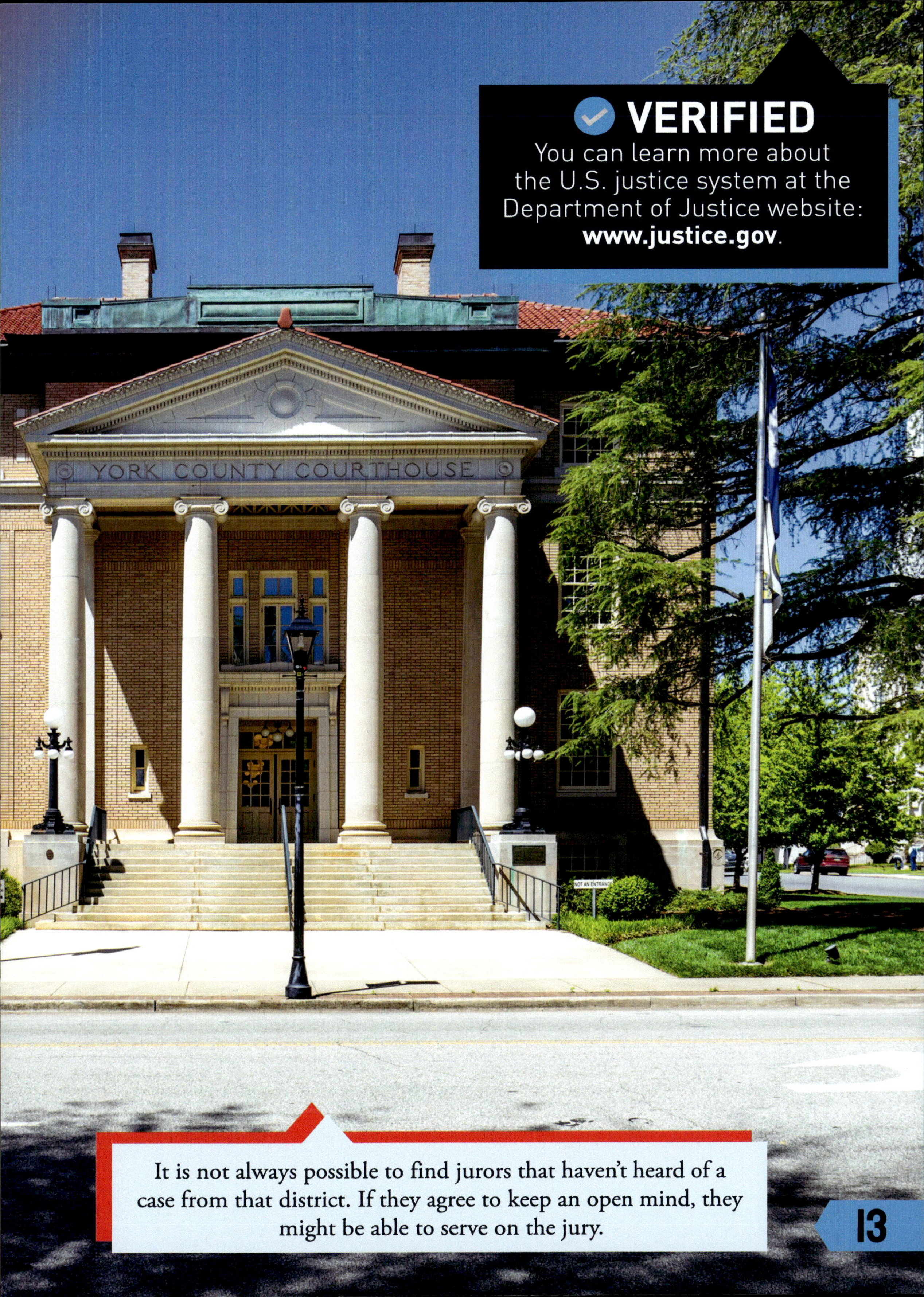

VERIFIED
You can learn more about the U.S. justice system at the Department of Justice website: **www.justice.gov**.

It is not always possible to find jurors that haven't heard of a case from that district. If they agree to keep an open mind, they might be able to serve on the jury.

Notice of Accusation

The next part of the Sixth Amendment gives people the right to know what they're charged with. If someone is accused of a crime, they need advance notice of charges so they can start to plan their **defense**.

It also gives the right to require witnesses to **testify**. This helps make sure people who are witnesses to a possible crime come to court and give their testimony, or their side of the story.

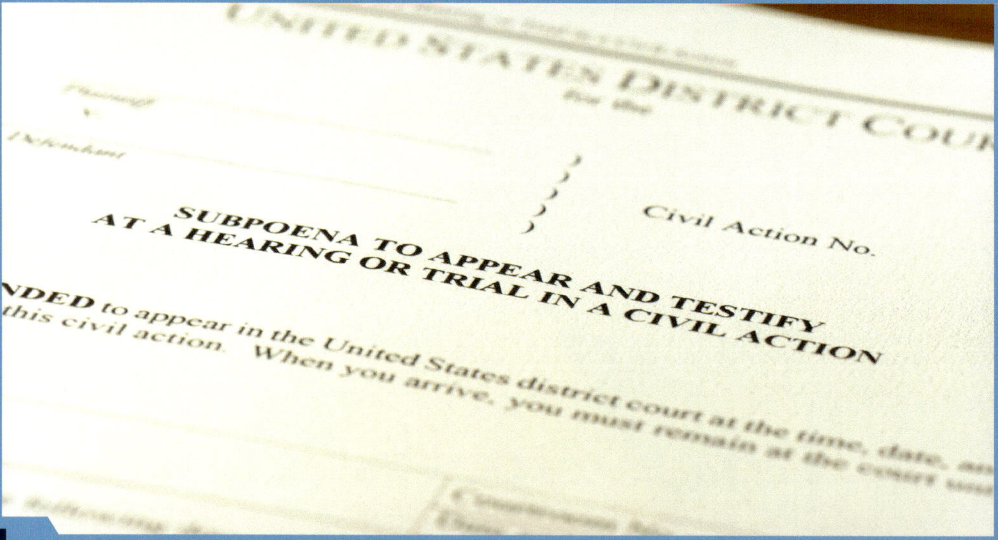

If someone may have witnessed a crime and needs to appear in court, the court sends them a subpoena. A subpoena is a legal document, or paper, that orders them to come to court and testify.

Confrontation Clause

The confrontation clause, or part, of the Sixth Amendment makes sure that the person being accused of a crime knows who is accusing them. It's important to know who is bringing a case to trial and to have the chance to ask them questions.

It also gives the right to **cross-examine** witnesses. This allows both sides to question witnesses and share their knowledge and evidence about the crime. Cross-examining witnesses can also help the jury decide whether there are weaknesses in the case against the defendant.

SUPREME COURT CASE

In the case *Pointer v. Texas* in 1964, the defendant didn't have the chance to cross-examine a witness. Instead, the court used the witness's testimony **transcript** from an earlier hearing. The Supreme Court ruled this was against the defendant's Sixth Amendment rights.

Being able to see witnesses in person is important for members of the jury. They can watch witnesses to decide whether they trust their testimony.

Compulsory Process Clause

The next part of the Sixth Amendment gives defendants the right to call witnesses in their defense. This is called the **compulsory** process clause.

This last part of the amendment gives people the right to have a lawyer to help with their case. A lawyer can help explain what it means if the client pleads **guilty**, so the defendant fully understands their rights. They also help with trial procedures, or processes.

In 1963, the United States Supreme Court decided that people charged with a **felony** would be given the right to an attorney, even if they can't afford one.

SUPREME COURT CASE

In the case of *Gideon v. Wainwright* in 1963, the defendant couldn't afford an attorney and asked for one to be appointed to him. He was denied, or turned down. The Supreme Court ruled that it's a constitutional right for states to provide legal help to defendants who can't afford to pay for it.

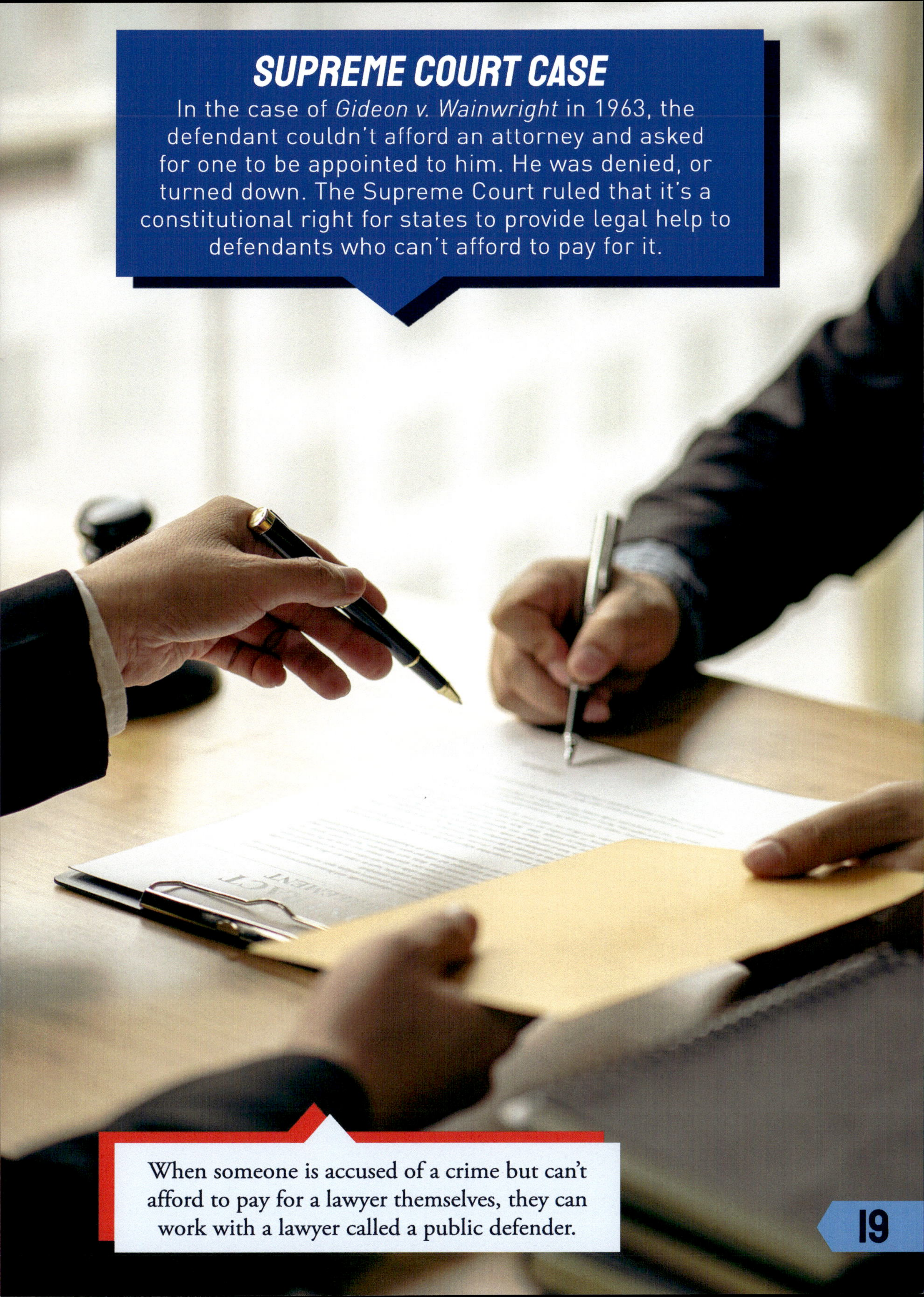

When someone is accused of a crime but can't afford to pay for a lawyer themselves, they can work with a lawyer called a public defender.

Criminal Cases and Civil Cases

A criminal case is when someone is accused of breaking a law and committing a public offense. If they're found guilty, they could go to jail.

A civil case is a **dispute** between two parties, or people. People in civil cases might file a lawsuit for money or to have something returned to them.

The Sixth Amendment doesn't give people the right to a jury in a civil trial case. However, the Seventh Amendment does.

Family cases, such as those to do with **divorce** and child **custody**, are also civil cases, but they don't have juries. They are heard only by a judge.

DIFFERENT TYPES OF CASES

Criminal – Includes a crime against the public or society. Examples: murder, robbery, kidnapping.

Civil – Includes a case between individual people or companies. Examples: harm to a person, harm to property, contract disputes.

Seventh Amendment

The Seventh Amendment guarantees, or promises, a trial by jury for certain civil cases that go to federal court. Most civil cases don't have trial juries. In fact, less than 1 percent of civil cases use a jury to reach a decision.

Most states also include the right to a jury for civil cases in their state's constitution. States also have different laws for which types of cases can be heard by a trial jury.

TWO SIDES OF A CIVIL TRIAL

Defendant
The person or party accused of committing some wrongdoing. They are trying to prove they're not guilty.

Prosecution or Plaintiff
The person or party accusing the defendant of the offense. They need to prove that the defendant is guilty.

VERIFIED
You can learn more about our justice system on the Office of Justice Programs website:
www.ojp.gov

The side that's accusing the defendant is called the prosecution in a criminal case and the plaintiff in a civil case.

The Jury's Job

A jury decides on a verdict, or outcome, for the case they hear. Members of the jury listen to evidence and decide whether someone should be found guilty in a criminal case. They decide which side will win the lawsuit in civil cases.

All jury members are asked to pay close attention during testimony and whenever evidence is presented. As a group, they meet and privately discuss, or talk about, the evidence that was provided. This is called deliberation.

During a trial, members of the jury sit in a special area of the courtroom called the jury box.

Deliberations

During a jury deliberation, the jurors talk about the evidence and proof they heard in court. They share their thoughts and opinions on the case. They are reminded to always be respectful of each other and not to try to force their opinions on anyone.

They can ask to look at the evidence again during this time. They can ask questions about the information that was presented to them. They can also ask to read the testimony they heard.

TAKE YOUR TIME

Jury deliberations don't have a set time limit. Members of the jury can take as much time as they need to try to come to an agreement.

Usually trials are public, but jury deliberations are always held in a private room. This is to make sure jurors can have open discussions about the case and share their opinions.

Making the Decision

For most criminal cases, the jury's decision needs to be unanimous. This means everyone agrees on one decision. For many years, Louisiana and Oregon didn't require unanimous decisions. However, in the case *Ramos v. Louisiana* in 2020, the Supreme Court ruled this was against Sixth Amendment rights.

If a jury can't decide on a unanimous outcome after much deliberation, it may be considered a hung jury or a deadlocked jury. A judge must make this decision.

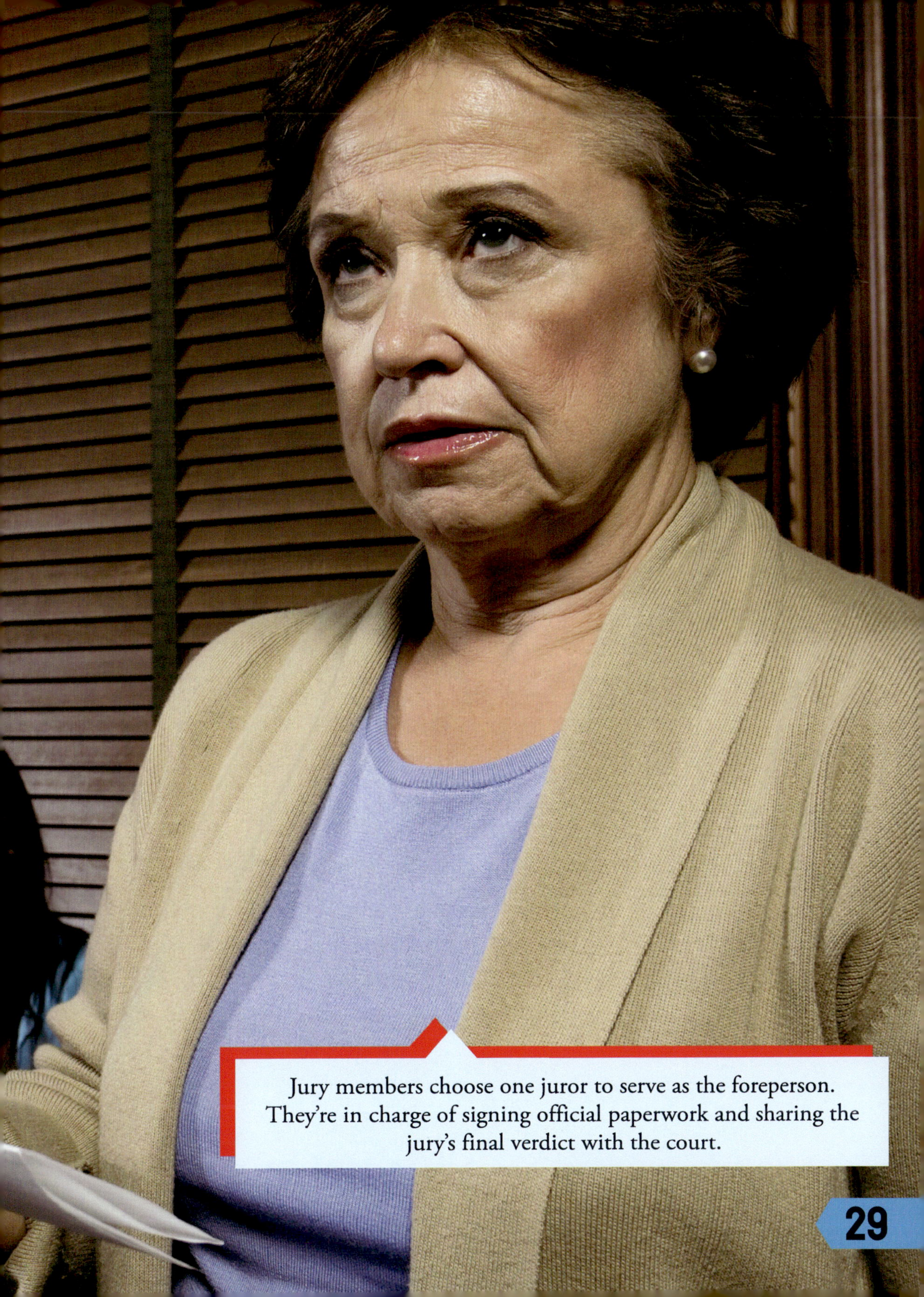

Jury members choose one juror to serve as the foreperson. They're in charge of signing official paperwork and sharing the jury's final verdict with the court.

The Verdict

After the jury reaches its verdict, the defendant on trial will be found guilty or not guilty. If they are found guilty, the judge will later give their sentence, such as jail time in a criminal case or a fine in a civil case.

A hung jury can lead to the judge declaring, or stating, a mistrial. This is a trial that isn't valid, or acceptable. Mistrials can also happen if evidence or testimonies are falsified, or faked, or improperly handled.

OUTCOMES OF A POSSIBLE HUNG JURY

- The judge may ask if jury members need more time to deliberate.
- The jury can ask questions for more information on the case.
- The judge may declare a mistrial.

VERIFIED

You can read transcripts for federal trials on the National Archives website: **www.archives.gov/research/court-records**.

If the defendant is found guilty, they may be able to appeal their case. An appeal is a review of an earlier decision in a lower court. The case will be heard again in a higher court called a court of appeals.

Serving on a Jury

You may know someone who's been called for jury duty. People get called to serve on a jury on a **random** basis depending on where they live. This helps make sure there are people with different backgrounds on the jury.

Possible jurors must go into the courtroom, and lawyers ask them questions. This is to find out if they can fairly judge the case. People might be **dismissed** if they have a reason to support one side of the case.

SPEAK THE TRUTH!

The process of choosing jurors is called "voir dire." This is French for "speak the truth." Lawyers from both sides speak to possible jurors and learn about their backgrounds and beliefs.

Every year, millions of people in the United States are called for jury duty. If you skip jury duty when chosen, you can get fined or even go to jail.

Important Responsibility

It is a **responsibility** of citizens to serve on a jury if selected. This is one way people can be a part of the government in their everyday lives.

Still, serving on a jury can be hard. You may not be able to work at your job for a certain time or receive your regular pay. You might need to spend time away from your family. However, although it can be hard, many people have said their time as a juror was informative and **rewarding**.

DOUBLE JEOPARDY

If a defendant isn't found guilty in a trial that isn't a mistrial, they can't be put on trial again for the same crime, even if more evidence is found. This is called double jeopardy.

Lawyers directly address the jury during the trial. Their opening statement explains general information about the trial. Their closing statement reminds the jury of evidence and sums up their side of the case.

VERIFIED

You can read juror experiences on the U.S. Courts website under "Jury Service": **www.uscourts.gov**.

Being Fair

Before there were protections for jury trials, the people making decisions on legal cases often knew the defendant. They sometimes used information they already knew about the person to make decisions. This could lead to unfair verdicts.

It's important that a jury is made up of people who don't already know much about the case. Everyone has different backgrounds and personal beliefs. Having a group of people who can listen to the facts and evidence helps give someone a fair trial.

RULES OF THE JURY

People on the jury aren't allowed to read newspapers or listen to news stories about the case while they serve on the jury. They may also need to be sequestered, which means they are **isolated** from other people.

Our justice system is based on the idea of people being "innocent until proven guilty." Trial juries help to assess, or figure out, guilt by using evidence and testimony from witnesses.

Jury Bias

Juries are very important to our democracy, but there are also some challenges, or hardships. For example, hearing evidence from witnesses about a crime can be hard for people to process. It can be hard for jurors to separate their emotions, or feelings, from the facts of the case, especially in difficult, or hard, cases.

Bias is another consideration. Members of the jury are asked to only use the facts presented in court and not opinions they already have. Jury members' own personal beliefs can still interfere with, or get in the way of, their decisions.

During jury selection, possible jurors are asked if they have any biases that may affect their view of the case. Biases can also be **implicit**.

other options

Not all cases are decided by a trial jury. In many civil cases, both sides will settle, or come to an agreement, before a case goes to trial. People in criminal trials may plead guilty to a lower crime to avoid going to trial. This means a jury wouldn't be needed.

There are also cases when a judge will listen to the evidence and give the verdict instead of having the case heard by a jury. This is called a bench trial.

BENCH TRIALS

Unlike jury trials, bench trials are not a constitutional right. If a defendant chooses to waive, or give up, their right to a jury trial, they may have a bench trial instead.

A plea **bargain** is when a defendant pleads guilty to a lower-level crime. This can mean they'll get a reduced sentence or certain charges might get dropped.

Changes over Time

The number of cases that are decided by a jury in the United States has gone down in recent years. Studies have shown that the number of federal criminal cases decided by jury trials went from 8.2 percent in 1962 to 3.6 percent in 2013.

ONLINE COURT

Another recent change in trials today is the use of computers to conduct court hearings. During the COVID-19 **pandemic**, many courts couldn't meet in person. Instead, they held sessions over the internet.

The Constitution gives the public the right to watch federal trials. You can visit a federal court in person or watch a live stream online.

Before going to trial, many defendants accept plea bargains or choose to settle out of court instead. Sometimes defendants choose to plead guilty to a lower-level crime rather than leave the decision to the jury.

Voice of the People

Jury trials have been a critical, or important, part of our democracy since the United States was founded over 240 years ago.

The Sixth Amendment and Seventh Amendment are meant to make sure people who are accused of crimes are treated fairly and that their rights are protected. Everyone has a constitutional right to have their case heard and to call in witnesses to help provide first-hand testimony.

Ideally, a jury is a group of one's peers that will hear the evidence about a case and will do their best to make an informed decision. Juries are made up of people with different backgrounds and experiences, which helps provide different viewpoints. Trial juries serve as the voice of the people in our legal system.

The scales of justice represent fairness in the legal system. It's important to weigh both sides of a case and the evidence provided to reach a verdict.

GLOSSARY

amendment: A change in the words or meaning of a law or document, such as a constitution.

aspect: A certain way in which something appears or may be regarded.

bargain: An agreement between parties that settles what each gives or receives.

bias: An attitude that favors one way of feeling or acting over any other.

compulsory: Mandatory, necessary.

convict: To find someone guilty.

cross-examine: The examination of a witness who has already testified in which to check the witness's testimony.

custody: Direct care or control over someone else.

defense: Something used in a court case to prove someone is innocent.

democracy: A government elected by the people, directly or indirectly.

dismiss: To refuse to hear or hear further in court.

dispute: A disagreement or argument.

divorce: The legal ending of a marriage.

evidence: Material that is presented to a court of law to help find the truth about something.

felony: A serious crime punishable by a heavy sentence.

guilty: Having done wrong.

implicit: Capable of being recognized but unexpressed.

isolate: To put or keep someone or something in a place that is separate from others.

pandemic: An illness happening over a wide area and affecting many people.

principle: A general or basic truth on which other truths can be based.

protect: To keep safe.

random: Showing no clear plan, purpose, or pattern.

ratify: To formally approve.

responsibility: A duty or task you're expected to do.

rewarding: Likely to yield a reward or other benefit.

sentence: The time in jail or the fine a convicted criminal receives.

testify: To speak or answer questions in front of an audience, such as a court of law.

transcript: A printed or written-out copy of a court case.

INDEX